Compatible Aspects of the Disparate Endeavor

I0152345

Felino A. Soriano

NeoPoiesis Press, LLC

NeoPoiesis Press
P.O. Box 38037
Houston, Texas 77238-8037

www.neopoiesispress.com

Comparable Aspects of the Disparate Endeavor
Copyright © 2011

Comparable Aspects of the Disparate Endeavor
by Felino A. Soriano
ISBN 978-0-9832747-2-8 (paperback : alk. paper)
        1. Poetry. I. Soriano, Felino A.

Printed in the United States of America

First Edition

For Gabriela, Deisy, Angel and April: the loves of my devotional disposition.

Contents

Introduction

How does one find harmony in an unequal endeavor? This is the question that Felino A. Soriano places before us in the title of his collection *Compatible Aspects of the Disparate Endeavor*. In this case the "disparate endeavor" is to find a relatable face within the painted lines and ink markings of paintings that, for the general layman, are faceless. How does one give a succinct voice to an abstraction?

What Felino A. Soriano does not do is leave us to interpret this foreign language by ourselves. The poet acts a skilled docent leading us through an unknown gallery, while also begging us to use our imagination to navigate our own subconscious as in the case of **- after Victoria Lenne's Fractured Reflections:** The behind us is an "us" of disastrous dimensions. / An us / coordinated with logic undefined / by fogless thought, / clarity / the lover / we selfishly neglected / to invite / and stay.

Within the hands of this skilled poet, the once unreachable task of finding a commonality within the lines of a painting somehow seem attainable as in the case of - **after Nell Milne's Fragmentation:** Something leaves, but stays momentarily. The shape of the sensed / shape, here until the eye blinks violently / killing the appearance of tangible existence.

What happens in the process of Soriano's use of white space (allowing us those small rooms to take breath within) and heavy enjambment is nothing shy of a transformation. Within the narrative we begin to see a semblance of ourselves, "can the background of a moment / teeming / with unrecognizable displays / conjure / in a mind purpose or fashionable want, / secrets to express what desire / hides in the pocket of the / infantile subconscious?"

It is in this process of genuflecting that the poems find buoyancy and transcendence. The poems step forward and take the place of paintings themselves on the figurative gallery walls. Soriano's poems are more than merely a bridge that connects us to the beating hearts these paintings. They are works of art themselves, whether fixed or free verse, lyric or language driven, traditional or experimental, they find a compatible aspect in the disparate endeavor of our own existence.

- Billy Burgos
poet/illustrator and radio show host

after Victoria Lenne's *Fractured Reflections*

Glass ahead already damaged, antiquated.
　　　　This
outcome
　　　　　　　lasts until
　　　　　　　　　　　mending hands
transforms future into
　　　　　　　serial occurrences
of the rearranged paradox.

　　　　　　　　　　Shift
　　　　　　　　　　　　the paradigm:
privileged, though the face
resembles
　　　　　　　specified gnarls,
　　　　　　　unlike the child's
smile
　　　　　　　whose light maintains posited heat,
thus the mother never leaves until he is sleeping calmly,
undisturbed.
　　　　　　The behind us is an us of disastrous dimensions.
An us
　　　　coordinated with logic undefined
by fogless thought,
　　　　　　　　　clarity
　　　　　　　　　　　　　the lover
we selfishly neglected
　　　　　　　to invite
　　　　　　　　　　　and stay.

after Nell Milne's *Fragmentation*

Paused	on the visionary	purple, pine
limbs		
housed	with specialized symmetry	encased in
tented		
shadows	bruised but by light's	extraordinary
exit		

not of physical intent to segregate into an isolated fever
                    causing emotions to spread a juxtaposed
fright/anger vernacular to the onlookers blinded to naturalized
beauty.

Paused, the turquoise coat of a dragonfly's attire, narrates
what gorgeous connotations describe in wordless lexicons,
for in what the eyes hold, taut, space inexistent

is what posits the cliché, in the eye of the beholder.

Something leaves, but stays, momentarily. The shape of the
sensed
shape, here until the eye blinks violently
killing the appearance of tangible existence.

        Left in the assembly line verdict proclamation of
routine
endeavors, we turn to memory to instruct intellectual overtures
leading to full-body reenactments that have properly
prophesied
arrangements of location will be scattered, thus
unrecognizable.

after Arfius Arf's *The Last City*

The last city
among the inhabitant fireflies
abstract collocation of light
and skeletal flight

too, will resemble dust, fragmented scent attached
to its barely breathing rose. Death
the coming angular spear

with determined dispositional goal. Citizenry
have already passed into the walking blind,
the unacquainted. Fright inexistent

fallacy brought upon civilization to crawl beneath
the dark belly of an obese calendared night. Moon's
last shine

sky's eye aware therefore mountain knuckles
rubbed elongated pupil into blood vessel burgeon.

Awaken will be missing. Sleep, the fundamental conscious
whose clarity will maintain vision after the last has
fallen into acclimated absence.

after Martin Salajka's *Water Sprite 01*

Discerning visual pattern moves one
to disclose in self a fear of unknown

                              the cliché
obstacle man places purposely on paths

to obtain routine from that of anxious, callused hands.
This creature,
lime in appearance missing from the lexicon
of believable tongues.

                    If approached
sans effective methods
the spirit can rise from the flesh soft water
into vanish-echo of butterfly

                         ensuing
the kiss of algebraic air.

Believing, subjective.

Can the background of a moment

                            teeming
with unrecognizable displays
        conjure

in a mind purpose or fashionable want,
secrets to express what desire
hides in the pocket of the
infantile subconscious?

after Chen Shuxia's *Fashion Face*

Faces are alterations
        revised into novel hypothesis
inferring the area of age
alive in the simple fathom
father has decided to decease
following last of official breaths, distanced
through ascension
collocated with
wit and apparent gift for etching
monotone memories.

Faces
made to reveal relevance, skin's
prior taut formations
now
        elasticized wrinkles, oh the good times
have jumped through
skyscraper's least
attainable window.

Faces find new homes
resting
within symptoms of aging
melodies, more precise after
following frequent sounds gone
to find newness, and the smiles
are born again, born into worlds
clashing, clashing prior to opening
importance.

after Jean-Michel Basquiat's *Untitled (Taxi Cab)*

He
commits carrying onto top shelf
substance, transporting
needing-more-than-ambulation
towards enigmatic and open-mouthed
locations. Silence
interrupts lips' obsessive
union,
and he, driver of absolute
cliché
delves into eyes unneeded of oscillation,
sending passenger free time
involving separation from past and
subsequent locations
reliving the in between freedom
of childhood's want and italicized
maturation.

after Marc Chagall's *Le coq dans le bouquet bleu*

Child unaware of
outside existence outside mother's
contoured cradle. Needn't anymore
bottle's calming cold
to finalize formation the
body no longer crawls.

Imagination runs.

Bodies exist of avalanching imagery.

Mother whispers

pretend, young one, your appeal is aggregated semblance
portending your eyes capture shapes priorly unseen, and
sounds incorporate sharper conveyance
outside the exterior womb
I have consciously created
to inhabit your ever growing
repetitious shadow.

after Elvira Bach's *O.T.*

I recall this form of guardian,
simplistic thorns
as day provides crawling irritation
terrace's height too high
the message better read
than attempting dismissing ascend.
She cultivated pause,
akimbo.
Her callused vision
interrogates sans language.
Wonder
is the encompassing query:
Beyond her tilting glare,
what behind her demands physical
touch,
calling towards the curious
unable to accelerate beyond
cyclic, medieval protection?

after Ranier Fetting's *Fraenkelufer*

As the white body, horizontal   dissipates
on inhale murder fantasized
study-destruction, cigarette
falters, forms evaporation-ghosts
shaping bodies of questions
alternating gray with geological
whereabouts. Her head
on the lowest portion
neck provides adequate strength, and withering
are among the thought-congregations
perched
near wires crossing brain's
chemical composition.

Upon opening
eyes near swollen among tears,
lake's sensitive side
blows into circulating strands of
acrobatic air a
ballad inducing memories,
meant to expand her serrated lips
into the smiling rendition
her mother always
promised to announce.

after Jörn Grothkopp's *Koi*

Koi produce
gilded desires
through weaving
threads of invisible
abstraction. Dressing numbers
rise in threes
written on orange peeled
backs inventing
ornamental movement.

Luck, not here, for the fish
revive substance without
conscious need
to dive behind pennies
expressing wishes
for the paranoid persons
blind to unhindered
appearances.

after Jane Kelly's *If We Could Undo Psychosis 2*

The could would inherit a smile wrap
-around the entire being. Your face now
aware of the unawareness to the open
empty book of illustrated absence

does not intertwine correctly with those
posing with you.

The if, question hybrid statement would bathe
constantly, redoing its body into fresh,
flattened concrete, foot and harm printless, unstained

say a flower silent in its sing toward sun
ears, brilliant blue or purple in the positive,
unbruised definition.

The greeters would do so without empathy.

Medication would be an other-reality, a non
hand staining ritual carving edible stones
atop the masticated tongue.

We would alert you, recall in the wandering
stilled mind a landscape of physical happiness,
similar to a stream's million eyes
illuminating the silver crusted fish
propelling the sky of crystal elucidation,
heading among the pointing plants
toward elsewhere where darkness only
exists at the proper, expected periods.

after Georgina Hall's *The Outing*

Mother conjoined by baby's grasp
unmistakable scent. Baby
conjoined by mother's awareness
distinctive hold.

Recall a standing ballad, a song demonstration
causing tear and mending thread to ascertain
emotional gardens trampled by feet of malevolence.

This though, only in the horrid aspect of isolation
separation.

Faceless known only by man-named mother, baby.
In a garden of passersby, perhaps the tongue of your voices
can identify you more brazenly, or in such a way the
beautiful connection of two formed specialized
body breaths

can mirror your reciprocating hold, a physical
proclaim face is unneeded in a world of blind
mediocrity.

after John Geggie's *Curious Child*

Imagination

the open
present prodigy collecting

abstract beings smaller than the
eye admits in their subjective

reality.

after Richard Cronborg's *Love Lost*

Because the arsonist lost faith in
keeping you warm. Shall the night
hesitate to form its white shaft
magazine spine inspired halo

you will sit enlightened

not in worldly manifestations,
the butterfly wrapping yarn
with golden dust circles atop
its wings,

—enlightened by the prodding sears
tears leave tattooing paths of emotion
down the almond form feature
of your swollen cheek.

after Mark Francis' *Mesh*

First light,
wind's accurate hands
draw back dusky threads,
night's difficult, darkened curtains.
Left, much. Much unfrozen
as thawing breath of morning's
effort releases, purifies. Not a window
unopened. All, visible, and fingers
free to trace an abstract, cursive
conversation across the board
sky holds without the clenched
anger of jealous hands.
Bodies bend, a branch's body bends.
Leaves released, a playtime solution
idea to name new death, dust
skeleton later, the leaves' decapitated
green. First light,
alphabet sky, lake neighboring
a frog's leap, hummingbird's
vanish. Conjoined, all, though
shapes differ, semblance of symmetry
watching the watching, allusion to
time when movement shapes aliveness,
allegorical existence.

after Philip Taaffe's *Untitled*

Pomegranate's pores,
seepage, opposite disgust
mends the tongue's torn
hankering among
sugar's name
                    and
sour's choking of taste buds,
relentless. This bloody fruit
stains the faces of smiling fingers.
Garments, safe
only
                in the advent of
partial or blatant protection
called removal
                    or
with precision slicing outer fruit clothing
        peeling results in a clean
departure.
                        Resting in bowls
of ceramic wombs
or
            kept cool by the stainless steel
box's
                incubating dialed breaths,

the seeded beginning becomes into
satisfaction
                on a day heat exhumes
                                            craving
of a carried devotional
outcome, subjective
                    terminology feeds
the mind's specialized
                    wants.

16

after John Saccaro's *Dreams and Lies*

A sleeping state
ersatz
           angles
articulating
           shapes

           mischievous
renditions   reality
never imposes while
ascertaining semblances

marbled in texture.
           Pathological
curiosity, a drawing
hand
           misinterpreting
the object akimbo or
sitting to command
a self
           diagnosed
differently
nightly,
           —such is the
fatal form of misunderstanding
night-born abstraction.

17

after Davis Rhodes' *Untitled*

When shapes
obscure
        sedentary
                senses,
the eyes unsheathed
                  focus, a firm focus
on outside lines
capable
            in the aspect of stilled portraits
to purchase familiarity,
                although
abstract is the fashionable
clothing
        tailored
            to outline
voyeurs' copacetic imaginary
timelines
        betwixt
death, and the prelude
           of birth's ongoing
dilemmas.

after Robert Gutierrez's *Let Evening Come*

For this gift
needn't be man-wrapped, hand-tainted,
                                        furthermore
                    misleading
the want
                    into reactionary nuisance
as
            the hiding beneath gilded paper
                                        reveals
a difference, a disposition
not aligned with
                    the opener's
invented emotions.

All is expected, naked, nude in its documented
vellum.
                    Dusk, its brand of cotton
                        falls
forms
                    on the land awaiting, daily
near the clock's
                        accurate voice
constructing a message of
evening, welcome.

after Mykola Zhuravel's *Musicians*

The challenge, to close
the mouth, the open eyes.
To feel the colors becoming
bodies,
the hand-poured from
horns' vibrating bells,
depicting concept, time,
turmoil, too, an imitation
of a lake's voice, whispering
into the singing bluebird's
rendition of "What a Wonderful World".

after Nguyen Dieu Thuy's *Colour of Passion*

Or, of the party
balloon
unfettered from
toddler hands,
becomes emancipated
momentarily,
a priori assumed
before the house's ceiling
engages in prisoner tactics
forming seal and shadow
of the rounded decoration,
dwindling after days of uncontrolled
attempts of failed
repossession.

Instead, though
of a rose's graceful blush,
her cheeks toned
to mirror a distance,
a distance resting on horizon's
plentiful table, a blend then
occurs
of which the eyes' hands pluck
and pull and plant these shapes
where the human hands follow
inside a metaphor of new
documentation.

after Beo Nguyen's *The Philosopher*

He
isolates in delineated function,
the naked from geometric abstraction

talking to summary of intelligent salvation. Answer

answer

the tongue's cohesive hankering.

Said to himself

"I do not understand the language of my neighbor,
but understand the vertical veracity
my hand-held yoyo
posits into a realm of
personal separation from time,
time.

after Mike Massengale's *Out of the Darkness*

Her strumming harmony
                    attacks
with winged liberation
ground-summary
erases
        upon
uttered failed deconstruction.
                            Her
instrument
vocalizes seismic
                    comprehension
sliding the blonde hair
of Autumn's nearing-end.

Listen,
her
                construct
the personal concept
imagination
struggles
                until
life within horizontal
movement

ignites first words
into summarizing
most-inner
                    contours.

after Sue Duda's *Crazy Fingers*

With elaboration
the birthed is often
subliminal.

We'll anticipate
vertical curves'

                concrete expansion

we'll analyze

pound

         pound
         pound echoes
humming
remorse for inexact narration

                        tongue
misquotes with adequate ease.

Fingers, the curled
tone of constant reverberating hail,
admit
to the watching fortune

jazz

        is the constant mirage
glazing the eye with unobstructed

rapture.

after Donald Maier's *Backyard and Birdhouses*

Because quiet
is the best suited body
to sit within embrace of white,
plastic
outdoor chairs, and the roaming beneath
feet with cataract sight
can roam within glare of green's slanted grass,
sectioning rooms
of the yard's most elegant,
dilapidated region.

after George Wesley Bellows' *Portrait of Emma in Night Light*

Her face was
stone
      afterward of precious
patterned devotion. Dangling
of silence's molding
a multiplying layer expanding

                          outward,
and her eyes
speak of written prose
priorly misunderstood
as voices often
facilitate
dedicated fantasies.

after John Leslie Breck's *Twilight on the Charles*

Sky
a purple
unpretty bruise methodology
dropping echoes of demeaning self
atop pond of acclimated tempos
man forgot
to separate into
existence more semblance
than the circle returning center point
embracing the embraced
in reverberating modes of
monotonous self-touching.

Later
sky a clarity of sound
with squawks contemplating
directional worth, shot
by man or by
many a reason called upon to
abscond in responsible
protocol.

after Jacob Collins' *Study for Bed I*

Wrinkles raised
as if several bodies
slide in contrast to stillness
                          silently
                                amid a bed's
white sand with swirls of
                    yellow contours.

No bodies here, as in the prison
where bodies are cataract with
                          specialized names
differing from those of birth
when behind vertical stillness
of steel's delineating dungeons.

Here
a body is a sleeping absence, an absence
elevated
                    above closed and dedicated eyes
whose hands reach from contours of
contoured lids
                    reaching
into the paradise of tousled sheets
explaining
a body once became its shadow,
lying in the tissue-dim light's open mouth.

after Silvia Gleisner's *Visión*

Of the sunburned hill habitual
uncovered dimensional
discovery, rediscovered happenings.
Bodies on site
                              away
from the visually curious.
Sitting
on lined palms of an outstretched
                                          fingertip
too far from nostalgia
as memory
cannot float
              where birds will not nest
among a heat
too overwhelming   too
elastic in its return
squeezing pleasure
from melodies of
cultivated happenings.

after Pilar Rios' *Momentos*

She wears
alabaster feathers on isolated wrist,
her orange
cloth draped on contours of brown skin
his hands
hold with desire of last exhales
wanting to return
atop lips sending necessary
farewell.

He with
wings of black
wrapped before flight
takes the body of moments
into halves of a self
crying into silence.

after Vilma Penrroz's *El Lechero*

With weight of the unfed
        thirsting
far beyond what can become
within naturalized sustentation.

Bottles of liquefied devotion
nutritional body tonic
                tumbling
of variations
        varied into delight   dancing
as to say gratitude to drink,
welcome
             welcome
the body is astounded.

after Paul Reed's *#19*

                                              Bodies
inter
          laced   forming
well-worn
fitted semblances
containing man-to-woman marriage
made of the sealed reality
                    unbroken distance
from catastrophic, neoteric normality

                                                  ending

love's loving cradle,
stronghold of mangled fingers
chain of circumstance
the never absent duo
of dissipating
                    singular cultivation.

after Irene Rice Pereira's *The Light of Spring*

And then the crow contains awakening. Window
an eye of blurred fog. Curtain's lengthy body
green creases kiss burgundy cloth
of dusty shoulders. Outside
cold fingers of a winter within spring
awakens before aliveness of mouth
captures auditory signals, morning's stretch
into semblance of pipeclay sky.

after Purvis Young's *Angel*

Happy man
conveys her identity,
handmade needing
unwrapping with
untying smile, name to which
brand is cliché
but
of the openly
sincere.

Angel sans documented halo,
her
voice of communal dedication,
he
voice of constant confirmation
transforms selfish loneliness
twisting into newness of elongated
braid of intertwining.

after Vasily Kandinsky's *Several Circles*

Several circles
        conjoined

                through
                involvement's
                iridescent
                womb
                awaiting
                birth's
        finality,
     amid
   texture's

realized devotional: it's time, time

for child to awaken into catapulted self.

after David Burliuk's *Sea View*

The burgeoning blue's open   hand
with particles of rippling
belief
          balancing on
softened palms. Near
edges of sound
distance
                    whispers return,
leaving
for the momentary sadness
glass bodies
                              falling
from the hand's
isolated, most dangerous edge.

after Jeff DOttavio's *Knots*

Bark's layered texture
crumpled paper method,
the design, abstracted culture   relevant
aspectual display. Vertical grain
quality
and if human, tree would run
from the definitional misdeed
tongues carve into air as
misfortunately hideous, yet
in the observing of beautiful reality,
tree's raised skin proclaims
a maturational construct
of the vertical expanse.

after Gerald Wartofsky's *Repose*

                           Away
in song of documented (near is chaos connoting algebraic
infinity)
solace
        near day's
                 fall
ing light of echoes
spelling names of myriad bodies

born into new fractions
signifying broken
               wholes.

                         She

a garden attire
scented rise-beauty her face-echo
calls toward empty room's
designated wish to
copacetic gather.

after Agnès Toulouse's *allee de peupliers*

Contemplation wears
each triangle skull on
trees' northern fathom.
Language of shadows
defines cultured spasms
shaking with snare drum rattles:

crumpled leaves

worm's prosthetic food
buys used space
residue of plagiarized past
evident

within last breath

leaves hypothesize
grace, grace.

after Barbara Steinacker's *After the Storm*

Sky   skeleton-silk,
surname: grand

positional [hang]
                        glide where hands
reach-can't causing
finger-traced slides
for weary birds'
weekend-joy.

after Lynda McDonald's *Dragon Lady*

Mimic unseen,   (mimesis faculty high-alert transform:
me-my-body)
        vanish.

                Voice-person, monologue
his shadow
                saddened, navy blue. Pardon
                                        excuse
my intolerance to chaotic verbs
running the spine of moments' con
stant
        shift.

                Those
call my disposition
                        predetermined scaly-flesh
fire from ontological
beginnings,

watch
                        as I describe
the shadow of circumference
lying body-still

design across
                fathom's self-indulgent portrait.

after Meredith Smith – Poczkalski's
The Heart

Organizes drum rhythms

                 strums

                           plucks

on

     allegory-paths

                love   malfunction

death if constant

engaged with improper guidelines
brain

       regards as elementary   survival.

after Willie McNeal's *Waterbird Reflection*

Morphs in blurred composition.

Walks away from standing still.

Hides
any function
hands may call toward graying walls:

dancing on glamour signs
one believes too much into his
selfish yen-constructs.

Such beauty, one-legged like stem holding wine's
loving clarity,
glass of wanting sip and angle-catching
light sans
biodegradable
blur.

after Alice Teichert's *Satin*

When sky is water, here
the memory is more functional (malleable
realization such substance eases around
corners of intellectual finality). We
slide on syllables, softly sounded
into proper pronunciation. Nothing
more elegant than crowning our lover's
frame, when sleeping. When she is
sleeping, the soft of her, the self of
her not awakened but breathing, this
satin cloth clothing her various
tones of collocated skins, resembles the name
we utter when beauty is the weight
balancing tongue with emotional
resuscitation.

after Ivo Stoyanov's *Interventions #1*

I queried of intervention
             when
invented storms are heavy
doses of medicating time.
        Who
finds ineffable segments of speech
   hiding
beneath cultures of
catastrophic dimensions?
The will to
find fortune in assistance.
Does treasure box open upon
manmade excavation?
                No,
then tell the arguers (storm | earth)
ceasing or continuation, bipolar
symptoms found among the alive
              no
longer can achieve the harmony found
within the blue jay's landing on
oak's welcoming gnarls.

after Sasha Rogers' *Place*

Place
is the open hand, the diagram of palm's
splaying lines
          finding
                    definitional humor in
                    leading
onlookers
          toward
relational advancements.
Horizon
is the calm species. The line
of this body, the constant line
outlining distance of which
                        travelling
cannot comprehend

unless
        imagination is the functioning
style
            open mouths utter with
fondling adoration.

after Raimonds Staprans' *Still Life with the White Box*

The usually wandering experiences, eyes',
the function of their selves find
absence the often chaotic irony
attached to memory's copacetic
device.

This white box dons lined bodies
near the armadillo's skin-raised
texture
       hands avoid from ersatz
empiricism. Population of sole
body
       box alive
fronting crimson walled interior
metaphors as screaming, "please
return", please
          for such an elongated absence
comforts only the self witnessing
delusion juxtaposed with the mind's
callous unawareness.

after Kristin Leachman's *Gravity Flow*

Home is the flame-conjure
moths of the human name return
upon discomfort. Re
                    turn
brings specialized triumph
not known until
                    fullness of the brick womb
beckons with softened adjectives,
                                    and the wandering
becomes well enough ascertained as
specific duty of consolation:
away's most unpredictable
scenarios.

after Squeak Carnwath's *Perfect Creatures*

Mind's forgetful praise for
messages objects project
sans reciprocation. Creatures
we *do* recall
correspond with anger's
diligence
                etched into why
hate so prevalent exists. No though
this type of candid speech
dissolves innately for the holders of
various creatures:

mother-vases with rounded hips
cupping lavender gifts with candy scents, and
                too
recall the holders of musical content
                    mirroring
wind's focus on reason
moving along paths of righteous delivery,
inviting lookers to comprehend their
spacious rhythms.

Permissions & Acknowledgements

I would like to gratefully thank the editors of *Radiant Turnstile*, *ken*again*, *The Sound of Poetry Review*, *Thirteen Myna Birds*, *Sugar Mule*, and *The Balloon* for kindly publishing some of the poems that appear in this collection.

About the Author

Felino A. Soriano (B. 1974) is a case manager and advocate for adults with developmental and physical disabilities. In 2010, he was chosen for the Gertrude Stein "rose" prize for creativity in poetry from *Wilderness House Literary Review*. Philosophical studies collocated with his connection to various idioms of jazz explains motivation for poetic occurrences. For information, including his 40 print and electronic collections of poetry (most recently *Differences of the Parallel Devotion*, Desperanto, 2011), over 2,500 published poems, interviews, and editorships, please visit his website: www.felinoasoriano.info

NeoPoiesis
a new way of making

in ancient Greece, poiesis referred to the process of making
creation – production – organization – formation – causation
a process that can be physical and spiritual
biological and intellectual
artistic and technological
material and teleological
efficient and formal
a means of modifying the environment
and a method of organizing the self
the making of art and music and poetry
the fashioning of memory and history and philosophy
the construction of perception and expression and reality

NeoPoiesis Press
reflecting the creative drive and spirit
of the new electronic media environment

www.ingramcontent.com/pod-product-compliance
Lightning Source LLC
LaVergne TN
LVHW091209080426
835509LV00006B/915